PATTERN FOR LIBERTY

PATTERN FOR LIBERTY

The Story of Old Philadelphia

by GERALD W. JOHNSON

McGraw-Hill Book Company, Inc. NEW YORK LONDON TORONTO

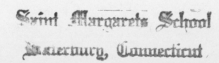

PATTERN FOR LIBERTY: *The Story of Old Philadelphia*

Library of Congress Catalog Card Number: 52–7451

THE ILLUSTRATIONS IN THIS BOOK ARE REPRODUCED THROUGH THE COURTESY OF CONTINENTAL DISTILLING CORPORATION, OF PHILADELPHIA, WHICH COMMISSIONED WELL-KNOWN AMERICAN ARTISTS TO PAINT THEM FOR DISPLAY IN NATIONAL MAGAZINES

Published by the McGraw-Hill Book Company, Inc.
Printed in the United States of America

To Philadelphians,

of the past

and the present,

for the future

THROUGH THE COOPERATION OF THE FOLLOWING ARTISTS

Frank Reilly

Simon Greco

James Bingham

List of Illustrations

PATTERN FOR LIBERTY

INSPIRED BY ENGLAND, BUT
NOT ENGLISH—INDEPENDENCE HALL
AS IT LOOKED IN 1800

PATTERN FOR LIBERTY

The Story of Old Philadelphia

"I SEE . . ." said the philosopher, pointing. He spoke in character, for it is the business of a philosopher always to see, and to see more than ordinary men; but his gesture was faintly comic, for he pointed at a chair. The others saw the chair, too, and you may see it tomorrow by walking into Independence Hall, in Philadelphia, where it still sits in the same place that it occupied in 1787. They all saw, as you and I can see, carved in the wood of the headrest a semi-circle with projecting rays, the wood carver's traditional symbol of the sun. But the man pointing at it that day was a philosopher who looked beyond the limits of other men's vision.

"I see," he declared, "a rising, not a setting sun." Because

NO INDIAN TROUBLES—
JAMES LOGAN, PENN'S SECRETARY,
CONFERRING WITH EQUALS

he was Benjamin Franklin, as amusing as he was wise, they laughed and cheered, and perhaps some of them saw with the philosopher's eyes. One hopes so, for the vision will outlast the chair, as the chair has outlasted the man. There are still Americans who, going through that national shrine, see it as the symbol of a rising, not a setting sun, and they laugh and cheer; and nothing fatal will happen to the United States of America while that is true.

On that day in 1787 they had just finished writing the Constitution, and Major William Jackson, secretary of the convention, was collecting and impounding every scrap of paper bearing any writing relating to what had taken place. He was under orders to destroy all of it, the official journal and the record of the yea-and-nay votes alone excepted. He carried out his orders so efficiently that historians have reviled him ever since; but it was the purpose of the Constitution makers never to reveal how violently they had disagreed or with what difficulty they had brought themselves to accept the instrument as we know it.

So there was tension in the air, although the long summer's work was done and all that remained was to wait for the engrossed copy of the document and sign it. Half the delegates gloomily expected to be repudiated by their constituents and have their work flung back in their faces. Even the imperturbable Washington, who had helped instigate the project in the first place, had presided over the deliberations of the convention, and was grimly determined that its labor should not be wasted, could say no more than that the event was in the hand of God.

Then up rose the ancient Benjamin Franklin, delegate from Pennsylvania, first citizen of Philadelphia the host city, philosopher, scientist, inventor, citizen of the world, but first of all, like one of his own lightning rods, a reliever of tension, a diverter of fearful potentials into harmless channels.

On the first day of the session, he said, he had taken note of the carving on the president's chair and it had occurred to him that, as represented by conventional wood carving, the rising and the setting suns look much alike. He professed that he was at that time not at all sure which would be the appropriate symbol for the convention then opening, but now he was assured that it was a rising, not a setting sun.

They laughed and cheered and probably didn't believe a word of it, but they felt better. We know that because so many of them remembered the incident long years later and recounted it as one of the high lights of the convention. But the curious thing is that the old philosopher, speaking lightly, spoke more truth than was contained in half the solemn, set orations of that laborious summer.

So the convention passed into history, and three years later Franklin, at eighty-four, was laid under a stone in an old churchyard two blocks from Independence Hall. But

FRANKLIN, THE FIRST CITIZEN
OF PHILADELPHIA WHEN STILL
ONLY ONE OF THE TOWNSMEN

the rising sun continued to climb, and Franklin of Philadelphia, could he return today, would scorn the American who would assert that it has reached the zenith yet.

"Franklin of Philadelphia" is correct, but inadequate. For all his Boston birth, he was in, and of, and for, and by Philadelphia. Adverse circumstances drove him away from Boston, but in Penn's town he found the environment that chimed perfectly with his temperament; he proceeded to remake Penn's town somewhat in his own image, but at the same time the town operated on him, molding him into its likeness. It is stealing the eloquence of a later Bostonian, but it is not distorting the truth to speak of Franklin and Philadelphia, now and forever, one and inseparable.

But Franklin was unique among American statesmen. To assert that he was the greatest of the time, of course, would be to start a long and inconclusive argument, for there is no

LIEUTENANT JOHN PAUL JONES
THRUSTS ASIDE THE BOSUN AND
HOISTS THE FIRST FLAG HIMSELF

final, conclusive definition of greatness; but he excelled all others in many respects. In 1787 Washington perhaps was as famous, but hardly more so; and no other American was regarded as being as learned as Franklin, or as versatile, or as shrewd, or as witty. No other statesman of the first rank was as ribald, either, and none as blandly independent of convention and propriety.

There may be some doubt as to the truth of the story that when the Queen of France extended her hand for him to kiss he gave her a hearty smack upon the lips instead, but Franklin is the only man about whom such a story was told, for neither Americans nor French would put it past him, and such presumption could not be imagined of any other man. In short, of all the Founding Fathers he was the most heartily, joyously, and shamelessly human.

In this he was a true representative of his town. It is a statement that may be challenged by those whose imagination paints Philadelphia always in Quaker gray, or by those without imagination enough to see it as anything except the industrial giant of modern times. But the little city that was, if not the cradle of American liberty, certainly its nursery and its kindergarten cannot be accurately portrayed in monotone.

From the very start Philadelphia was variegated and to some extent self-contradictory. Its origin lay in the desire of a seventeenth-century king to do something for a friend without seeming to do anything; and this friend was himself a strange combination of courtier and moralist, of shrewd businessman and romantic idealist.

Sir William Penn, soldier, sailor, and empire builder, had earned the gratitude of England, and his son, also named William, knew how to collect. Admiral Sir William had helped win at least two great naval victories and, as commander of an expedition to the West Indies, had given the empire Jamaica, one of the richest treasure houses among the colonies. William, his son, therefore deserved consideration; but many who deserve it never get it. William did.

Nearly three hundred years later what the world remembers about William Penn is his piety. It was genuine, without a doubt, but it was no more genuine and no more remarkable than his diplomacy. Rigidly austere in his own conduct, he yet contrived to remain on excellent terms with Charles II, the complete cynic, which is astonishing; but what is dumfounding is that at the same time he remained on equally good terms with the Duke of York, later James II, the complete bigot.

Penn was an exception to all rules, and somehow he transmitted something of his protean character to his colony. The world remembers the difference between his approach to the Indian inhabitants and that of the Spaniards and most of the English. To nearly all the European settlers, the Indians were part of the natural fauna of the region, no doubt higher on the scale of life than the fur-bearing animals but nonetheless to be exploited for the benefit of white men. Penn, almost alone, approached them as landed proprietors with economic rights that had to be respected.

It was a highly successful approach. The deal that was

made under the famous oak tree was perfectly straightforward, completely understood by both sides, and with no trick clauses in fine print. Penn executed his part of it to the letter, and, to the incredulous amazement of other colonies, so did the Indians. As long as William Penn lived, there were no Indian troubles in Pennsylvania.

Equally successful were the Penns' dealings—involving William and his heirs—with their white neighbors and rivals. Navigation and surveying instruments in the seventeenth century were far from precise accuracy, and Penn, doubtless in all good faith, planted his town a few miles below, instead of a few miles above, the fortieth parallel of north latitude, which was Lord Baltimore's northern boundary.

Much building had been done before the position of the line was determined accurately. Baltimore had brought suit and apparently he had a good case, but the Penns' diplomacy was equal to the emergency. After all, what were a few miles of wilderness among English gentlemen, even though one group were Catholics and the other not only Protestants but Protestants of one of the most extreme sects? The Barons of Baltimore eventually abandoned the contest.

The significant point in all this is that Philadelphia at the beginning was founded on the rule of reason.

William Penn was a Quaker who went to jail rather than abandon his faith, but in matters not connected with religion the kings of England found him to be an eminently reasonable man. Even in religion he was capable of understanding their position. He realized that they reigned over fanatical subjects and therefore could not seem to countenance the establishment of a colony dedicated to what the majority regarded as rank heresy. Penn, therefore, cheerfully agreed to the rule of religious tolerance in Pennsylvania, and this stamped upon the colony a respect for reason that prevented its drift into fanaticism of any kind.

No wonder that Benjamin Franklin, a hundred years later, found there an atmosphere congenial to his own utterly reasonable spirit.

Penn's interview with the Indian chiefs, in spirit if not in form, was the direct ancestor of the American Philosophical Society; for it was a gathering of men intent upon examining the world as it was. They hoped to arrange a way of living that would allow them to exist together amicably in spite of their differences, and that would permit each race to profit by the other's presence—which is essentially what Franklin had in mind in organizing the Philosophical Society.

The spirit of the founder of the colony was sustained and reinforced, as the years passed, by the geographical and economic position of the city. The thirteen colonies had only one important dimension, length from north to south, so Philadelphia, although on the seaboard, may fairly be called close to the geographical center of the country. So placed, it became the first great American—not national, for there was as yet no nation—trading center. It was a capital before there was a country, the financial and commercial, although not the political, capital of the colonies.

In this capacity it was essential for Philadelphians to familiarize themselves with the resources and needs, and thus with the ideas, of all the divisions of America. Fortunately, it is as true that familiarity breeds understanding as often as it breeds contempt. Philadelphia catered to Georgia and to Massachusetts, hence was at some pains to remain on good terms with both and with all the colonies between them. Thus it came about long before the Revolution that men from the extremities of the country meeting in Philadelphia felt that they were meeting not merely on neutral but on friendly ground.

So it became the natural place for serious consultations in stormy times. When Franklin made his remark about the rising sun, he was standing in what was already a hallowed spot, for in that very room, eleven years before, he had par-

COMMITTEE EXAMINING THE
RECAST LIBERTY BELL, CRACKED AGAIN
WHEN JOHN MARSHALL DIED

ticipated in framing the Declaration of American Independence. There the Continental Congress had met, except when it was driven away by the approach of a hostile army.

To some extent, it was also a desecrated spot, for there the enemy had held high revel when his troops were in possession of the American capital and the candle of American hope guttered and burned low. But in triumph or disaster, in accomplishment or frustration, Independence Hall was part of the fabric of American history.

Yet because the events connected with Philadelphia were of such vast significance and the problems with which statesmen wrestled there were so formidable, later generations have become accustomed to regard the early city as a solemn, not to say a somber, place. Nothing could be further from the truth. The Honorable Edward Rutledge, coming up from polished Charleston, and the Honorable John Adams,

CAESAR RODNEY ARRIVES
WITH THE DECIDING VOTE FOR THE
DECLARATION OF INDEPENDENCE

coming down from austere Boston, found it, one delight-fully, the other scandalously, gay.

For this very reason, its first citizen was not permitted to write the Declaration of Independence. In 1776 Benjamin Franklin was by long odds the most celebrated literary man in America and, indeed, the only one whose writings were familiar to any considerable number of Europeans; so it would seem that he was the logical choice for the task of phrasing a document of the utmost importance. But he was passed over in favor of a young, and then relatively un-known, Virginian named Thomas Jefferson.

Members of the Congress realized that this called for some explanation, and they were ready with it. Franklin, the in-carnation of Philadelphia, was, to be sure, master of a magic pen, but members could not rid themselves of the fear that if he were entrusted with the drafting of the Declaration he would put a joke in the middle of it. It is not unlikely that he would have done just that, and it is highly unlikely that he could have attained the eloquence and power that Thomas

Jefferson reached, so the decision was a fortunate one.

At the same time, it is a matter of some importance to avoid the error of thinking that the childhood of the republic was a sad one or even a consistently serious one. It is an error that may contribute to a misconception of modern America; for unless one understands the qualities of the people who made the republic, it is difficult to understand their work.

They were blithe, optimistic people. This may seem a strange way to characterize that model of rectitude and devotion to duty, George Washington, or that vinegary commentator on the total depravity of man, John Adams, or even that alert and agile business opportunist, Robert Morris, but it is true. These men attained the height of their fame when they were middle aged or elderly, and it is as they were then that we remember them; by that time labor, frustration and heavy responsibility had sobered them as they sober all men. But in the days when Philadelphia was the political, as well as the social, commercial, and intellectual center of the country, they were all, except Franklin, relatively young.

So were the city and the country—young, brisk, confident. This spirit contributed to what was done as surely as the wisdom, civic virtue, and courage of the Founding Fathers.

But to realize this clearly enough to give it its proper weight is not easy because it does not appear in state papers, and still less in the pages of historians, many of them solemn fellows unable to distinguish between good humor and levity, and nearly all of them in thrall to documentation. The spirit of the time is not to be discovered even in private correspondence, but is only to be deduced from it, for letter writers are, as a rule, concerned with events and with attitudes differing conspicuously from those of the majority. What everybody thinks and feels needs no reporting; yet it is precisely what everybody, with the usual few exceptions, thought and felt in the early days of the republic that could be most valuable to us in explaining how the country came to be what it is.

Fortunately, Philadelphia has records not confined to state papers or to written documents of any kind. There is enough of the physical city remaining—centering, of course, upon Independence Hall, but including many other buildings of the period—to permit, in combination with maps, plans, drawings, and other representations, a plausible reconstruction of the environment in which the young republic grew from swaddling clothes to schoolboy garments. And there are enough unofficial records to give at least a suggestion of its atmosphere as well as its architecture.

To begin with, Philadelphia was metropolitan. To say that of a town of 28,522 people (the population reported by the census of 1790) may seem an absurdity now, but it can be sustained by evidence. Indeed, a good argument may be made in support of what many would consider a greater absurdity, namely, that it was more genuinely metropolitan in 1790 than it was when the census of 1950 gave it more than two million inhabitants, with nearly as many more living in its immediate environs.

For "metropolitan" doesn't mean enormous, it means important. Specifically, it means important to the region in which the metropolis is situated. It means the city that leads all the other cities and towns belonging to the same group, not merely commercially but in the realm of ideas as well as in that of business.

In the period between the Declaration of Independence and the removal of the political capital to Washington in 1800, the primacy of Philadelphia in America was beyond dispute. For one thing, it had been until recently by far the largest city in the country, although in 1790 New York had forged ahead by five thousand. Its contacts with Europe were more frequent and more extensive even than those of Boston. Boston imported theology and Charleston theatricals, but Philadelphia imported both in quantity. New York exported furs and Baltimore flour, but Philadelphia handled both. Above all, it was both an importer and an exporter of ideas to a larger extent than its rivals because it was hospitable to any sort of ideas. A shoe buckle or a syllogism cast in an entirely new form could alike count upon examination with tolerant interest in Philadelphia, the first by the dandies on Market Street, the second by Dr. Franklin and his colleagues in the American Philosophical Society. Tom Paine was read in the city, but Edmund Burke was not neglected. A singer, a saint, or an acrobat could draw a crowd there—although not the same crowd.

For Philadelphia was the common ground, the meeting place of the extremes and, like the Athenians of St. Paul's day, its citizens delighted in nothing more "than to tell or to hear some new thing." Stern moralists, whether from Bradford's Massachusetts, or from Oglethorpe's Georgia, of course denounced it for its levity; but it pursued its cheerful way, busy, tolerant, interested and interesting, and the rest of the country, however it might grumble, was impressed and more often than not fell in line.

In addition to being metropolitan, Philadelphia was also new and, in this respect, unique among its kind. The metropolis of every other country stood upon the ruins of earlier cities, frequently upon many of them, and while it might possess venerable and wonderful monumental structures, it was always defaced by hideous remnants of the barbarous past. But every European visitor to Philadelphia was struck by the neatness of the little town, not yet broken and begrimed by the passage of centuries.

This must have added materially to the cheerfulness of the place in those early years—and cheerful surroundings tend strongly to beget confidence. Philadelphia was new; its history was all ahead of it, and cheerful men were bound to take a cheerful view of the future.

Finally, Philadelphia was strong, and knew it. True, during the seven years' fighting after 1776, its confidence in its strength was rudely shattered, for the enemy army swept in. Still, although a port, it was captured by an army, not by

THE HOME-TOWN BOY WHO
MADE GOOD—FRANKLIN RETURNING
FROM EUROPE IN 1786

a fleet. The heavy artillery of the time could command the Delaware and deny access to anything afloat. Sea power alone was, and is, unable to reach Philadelphia.

And it was the chief city of a strong country. In 1776 that country offered battle to a much stronger foe, but one unable to bring his full strength to bear; for the seas in 1776 were still barriers, not, as they are today, the most convenient highways for delivering military power at any desired point. In manpower, the colonies were inferior to Great Britain, but not hopelessly inferior. As far as population is concerned, the odds now are almost exactly reversed; yet for the United States today to undertake the invasion and conquest of Great Britain would be militarily a very serious thing indeed. In theory, perhaps, it might be done, but no rational American cherishes the delusion that it could be done swiftly or easily.

INTERESTED IN EVERYTHING,
PHILADELPHIA STAGES THE FIRST
AMERICAN AIR FLIGHT

By 1791, when it became the seat of government for the next ten years, the confidence of Philadelphia was, of course, unbounded. The War of Independence had been won; the loose confederation had been welded into a firm union; the material wealth of the continent had been to some extent revealed, but as yet was hardly touched. The future of Philadelphia was literally boundless, and if a typical Philadelphian attending Franklin's funeral the year before thought of his remark about the rising sun, he might have been excused for remarking, not "What prophetic vision," but, instead, "The poor old man—if he had only guessed the half of it!"

The Philadelphia of Franklin, and of the first ten years of the republic, the decade following Franklin's death, was something of an annoyance to British visitors because of the difficulty they found in describing it. The town was very obviously English, and yet not English. The difference was felt by everyone; yet no one could pin it down in words. This difficulty irritated many of the early visitors to the point at which they wrote peevishly about the place; yet they cannot be severely blamed, for to this day the essence of Americanism never has been clearly defined in words, and lack of a clear definition has led to countless misunderstandings.

Not only the character of the inhabitants but the very architecture of the place was affected. The building that was the center of the city's political life, the one now known as Independence Hall, is as certainly English in its inspiration as a building well could be; yet there is about it a sort of displacement of values marking it off from the true English Georgian.

Independence Hall was begun by the Province of Pennsylvania to serve as what we would now call the State House. In the 1730s Pennsylvania was feeling its importance as the richest and most populous of the American colonies, and it desired a building not only adequate to the transaction of provincial business but also imposing enough to impress strangers.

The task was taken over by Andrew Hamilton. The conventional statement would be that the task was "entrusted" to him, but people didn't entrust tasks to Andrew Hamilton —he simply took over as, some years later, he took over the defense of Peter Zenger in New York, and in a single jury speech established both the basis of freedom of the press and the reputation for subtlety of the Philadelphia lawyer.

When Hamilton was through, Pennsylvania had a capitol Georgian in its dignity and restraint, but un-English in its placid disregard of ascending orders. Both within and without, the horizontal lines are the emphatic ones in this structure. Everything is on the same level. There is nothing suggesting a throne room in which the eye is led upward to a culminating point at which Authority sits, raised above the people. In the legislative hall a low dais gave the presiding officer and the secretary enough height to see all the members and be seen by them; and the tower and spire rising above the roof constitute a mere accent, a flourish, graceful enough, but entirely dispensable.

The creator of Independence Hall was something of a mystery man. Nothing is known of his origin. He simply showed up, already an adult, in Accomac County, Virginia. We don't even know that Hamilton was his real name; but he picked up a rich widow in Virginia, picked up a six thousand-acre estate in Maryland, picked up a law degree at Gray's Inn in London, and picked up a tremendous law practice in Philadelphia. In his leisure moments he ran Pennsylvania, to a large extent, as recorder of the city and prothonotary of the supreme court, as member of the Assembly from Bucks County, and, on occasion, as representative of the proprietors. Nobody liked him, but everyone admired his independence and his ability, which made him something close to the Indispensable Man.

There is much of Andrew Hamilton in the building he designed. Exactly how it got that way is as obscure as its architect's early life, but the bland assurance of the lawyer is all there, as well as his extraordinary functional efficiency. Like him, it provides no place for either king or high priest.

Like him, it has absorbed much of the wisdom and grace of earlier times and other nations, but, as certainly as Hamilton defending Zenger, it puts its own interpretation on law, tradition, and precedent, thereby irritating pedantry. English in inspiration, Independence Hall is never more right than when it is wrong, from the traditional standpoint, and so becomes subtly un-English.

What was true of architecture was even more conspicuously true of social life in Philadelphia. English manners and customs were its basis, but English convention had to be adapted and modified to fit the new environment.

This necessity was frequently mistaken for ignorance by shallow-minded visitors, who assumed that the Americans, and specifically the Philadelphians, were trying to copy English manners exactly but didn't know enough to proceed correctly. But Lord Chesterfield could not have lived in Philadelphia exactly as he did in London for the simple reason that England was heavily and America thinly populated. In a heavily populated country, the ruling class may pick and choose its membership with a high degree of exclusiveness, but where the population is thin no talent may safely be discarded, for all must be used for all they are worth merely to maintain standards of civilized living.

For instance, London almost certainly would have turned a cold shoulder to Andrew Hamilton, for London had plenty of architects, executives, and astute lawyers whose origins were well known. "The career open to talent" was not a necessity where talent abounded; but where it was rare its value multiplied many times.

Philadelphians became expert in recognizing it. Robert Morris, the great shipping magnate, for example, knew sailors. It was a case of necessity. He had to know them—and merchants and factors, too—in order to keep his highly perilous business solvent. So when war began and it became plain that the new nation must make an effort on the seas, while the Adams cousins were pressing the claims of New England sailors whom they knew, Morris took a searching look at a down-at-the-heels seafaring man who appeared

~~~~~~

out of nowhere. Morris made up his mind that, however dubious his past, this was the kind of sailor the new navy needed, and got him a commission, not as a captain but as first officer on the *Alfred,* by courtesy called a "frigate," although she was not much of anything as a warship. While she lay in the Delaware the newly adopted national ensign was sent down, and when the order was given to hoist it for the first time, the second-in-command ordered the boatswain aside and handled the lines himself. Morris had not mistaken his man, for the sailor was John Paul Jones.

The appearance of characters such as these, and the necessity of using them for important work, gave to society in the new country a fluidity that visitors from more settled communities frequently mistook for instability. The idea that the treatment customarily accorded a gentleman should be

THE PREDECESSOR OF THE
STREAMLINER—THOMAS LEIPER'S
EXPERIMENTAL RAILWAY IN 1801

extended to a person whose grandfather nobody knew was simply beyond the grasp of eighteenth-century Europe. Yet there was no question that certain circles in Philadelphia lived a very agreeable life, even though they associated with wholly uncertified individuals such as Andrew Hamilton and John Paul Jones, or with others whose origin was all too well certified, such as that other Hamilton—Alexander—identified by John Adams as "the bastard brat of a Scots pedlar," or the ink-stained printer Benjamin Franklin. In short, society existed under conditions that Europe thought precluded its existence. It was English in its outward manifestations, yet most un-English in spirit; it was a mystery and, to many visitors, an annoyance.

Yet gentlemen in Philadelphia knew how to dine and ladies in Philadelphia knew how to dance. About that there was no debate. Furthermore, there were some in both sexes

LONG BEFORE ROBERT FULTON,
JOHN FITCH STEAMS UP THE
DELAWARE RIVER AT PHILADELPHIA

who knew how to talk, and while Philadelphia was the national capital these were augmented by temporary residents. Even after Franklin's death, the city held, for a large part of the time, two of the best conversationalists in America in Thomas Jefferson and Abigail Adams.

One of the most extraordinary temporary residents of Philadelphia during this period has left us one of the most extraordinary tributes to the American spirit of the time. Charles Maurice de Talleyrand-Perigord, expelled from France and then from England, fled to America, where he lived two years. Later, he said that the most astonishing thing he saw in this country was a lighted window that he observed as he was coming home at midnight after a party. It was in the house of Alexander Hamilton, and Talleyrand knew that it meant that Hamilton, after spending the day at the office as Secretary of the Treasury, was sitting up at night doing private law work to augment the slender salary the republic paid him. It was incredible, said Talleyrand, that a man through whose hands millions were passing, a man who had made the fortune of a nation, should have to labor late into the night to feed his family.

But it was not incredible to Philadelphia, for the city was accustomed to such inconsistencies. There was, for example, Robert Morris who, had he lived in Amsterdam, or London, or Leghorn, or any other great European commercial center, might have left a reputation only as one of the great moneygrubbers of all time. Even in Philadelphia he had accumulated what was then regarded as a great fortune. But his riches did not attach him, as wealth attached so many others, to the established order. When the revolt came, he flung into the patriot cause everything he had, not only his money but his time, his talent, all his energies, and even his neck, which the British would gladly have stretched on the gallows. This he did without hesitation, without compulsion, without holding anything back—and charged the country a whacking commission for so doing!

Robert Morris was unquestionably one of the great patriots of the era, and he was also one of the very few men who came out of the war enormously richer than he was when it began. He believed in America and, being a speculator, he gambled on what he believed in; but whether that makes him a member of the nobility or merely one of Fortune's darlings is a problem that, while it might have fascinated the quondam Bishop of Autun, held no particular interest for the Philadelphia of the early nineteenth century.

For the belief was characteristically American. We know that Washington, Adams, and Jefferson held it, but we are prone to forget that it was held also by the butcher, the baker, the candlestick maker—the little people, as well as the great. Benedict Arnold had it, but lost it, and that is when he began to turn traitor. Aaron Burr had it and retained it, but he tried to turn it exclusively to his own use and behoof, which was an offense of a different form from Arnold's, but still treachery. If we know that great villains were full of blithe confidence in the future greatness of the country, it is reasonable to assume that little villains might have shared that faith.

The Royalists testify to the fact. Their letters and journals are filled with bitter asseverations that the Continental army was loaded with rapscallions of every type—light-fingered gentry, horse thieves, runaways, and even blacker offenders. It is prejudiced testimony, certainly, but for all that it is probably true in part. Wars are seldom fought and won by the wholly irreproachable; and when the ranks are thin, no commander, not even one as austere as George Washington, is going to reject a good rifleman merely because he may have served a term in jail.

The people who conspicuously lacked this belief were the Royalists. Philadelphia had them, many of them in high places, beginning with the proprietors, the Penns themselves. True, John Penn, the last lieutenant governor under the proprietary, seems to have been a pretty faint Royalist. He formally adhered to the King, and was even imprisoned for a time in 1777, but the patriots never brought any serious charges against him, and he refused to leave, dying peacefully at Lansdowne, his estate on the Schuylkill, in 1795.

~~~~~~

But a considerable number of Philadelphians were less philosophical. Many who considered themselves the better element, and who certainly were among the better educated and better-off element, not only refused to accept the new order but collaborated enthusiastically with the army of occupation when the British captured the town. Naturally, this provoked retaliation, and it was rough, as judged by the standards of that time. In many cases it amounted to banishment and confiscation. That is rather gentle punishment for quislings in our more barbarous era, but at the time of the Revolution it was terrific.

The number of Tories who fled when the revolt succeeded ran into the thousands, but the number was less important than the selective quality of the purge. In any such political convulsion, the rich and comfortable are more likely to stick to the old order, and the poor and distressed more likely to be in favor of a change, so a heavy proportion of the American *émigrés* consisted of people who had enjoyed every material advantage.

There is no doubt that the wrath of the successful republicans deprived all America, and specifically Philadelphia, of much learning, culture, and social grace. Among the exiles were scores and hundreds of able and honorable men whose talents might have been very useful to the new nation. For this reason, some historians have described the expulsion as definitely a misfortune, almost a calamity to the United States.

But this estimate does not take into account the fact that these people, for all their virtues, were fainthearted and doubtful, therefore an element of weakness in a nation that had to struggle for survival against great odds. Belief in the future of America was the distinguishing characteristic that marked off potential citizens from unalterable colonists. Some of the Tories were very good people and admirable Englishmen, but they were not American, and the test showed that they were incapable of becoming American. So the loss of their energy and ability was not a net loss; the country was rid of their pessimism and skepticism, too.

〜〜〜〜〜〜〜〜〜〜〜〜〜〜〜〜〜〜〜

The elimination of the doubters and the objectors among the more influential must have contributed materially to the cheerfulness of the little city when George Washington and John Adams were its first citizens. They were not cheerful. They had the task of directing the new nation along a dark and perplexing course, which made them harried and apprehensive men. But even the sternest moralist is somewhat affected by his environment, so it is reasonable to assume that the first two presidents would have felt even worse had they been obliged to do their work in a gloomy town—say Halifax, where large numbers of Tory refugees gathered to prophesy, after the fashion of refugees, ruin and immeasurable woe.

The influence that the optimism of the city may have had upon the early history of the United States is not to be meas-

AN EXAMPLE OF THE
GREAT PERIOD—
THE BANK OF THE UNITED STATES,
WHICH LATER BECAME GIRARD'S

ured but, in Bacon's words, "is not beyond conjecture." There must have been many occasions on which a worn and worried President, at the end of a long day, found in some Philadelphia gentleman's home music and laughter and briskly confident conversation; and the President must have been more—or less—than human if the good cheer had not somewhat revived his drooping spirits, somewhat stimulated his faith, somewhat stiffened his determination. And that this was to the benefit of the nation none can doubt.

For the national government that came to Philadelphia in 1790 was still chaotic. Even its capital was not yet determined. President Washington had been inaugurated in New York, but Congress six years before had voted for the creation of a new, Federal city somewhere so that the government should not be the possession of any particular state. Since the Northern and Southern States could not agree,

HOWE WAS COMING IN 1777, SO THE LIBERTY BELL WAS TAKEN TO A PLACE OF SAFETY

Philadelphia was named as the temporary capital until a compromise could be worked out.

But the government that moved to Washington in June, 1800, was fixed and determined in its main outlines, which still exist much as the first two presidents shaped them in Philadelphia. Here Washington put the capstone on his work and earned his title of Father of His Country; for winning the War of Independence was not more important than guiding the first steps of the new government toward an assured place in the family of nations. It was Washington as President who established the ideals of dignity and probity that are worthy of a great nation—and he did it in Philadelphia.

Although John Adams considered himself, and is generally considered, a failure as President, he did one great thing. That was in 1798, when he refused to allow a storm of popular indignation to drive the nation into an ill-considered war with France. Under the Constitution the President is charged with the conduct of foreign affairs, and he assumed charge, in defiance of a raging Congress. By so doing, he saved the United States from the fate of all earlier democracies, that of failing in stability against waves of emotionalism. And he did it in Philadelphia.

A century and a half later, it seems fantastic to imagine that the government of the United States ever could have been overthrown by a mob, but it didn't seem fantastic to John Adams and his contemporaries. On the contrary, up to their time it had been the usual fate of democracies and the not uncommon fate of monarchies. The main reason for seating the national capital in a new city controlled by the Federal government was to eliminate all danger that Congress, the President, and the Supreme Court might be overawed by a city mob; and the modern motorist driving through Washington and cursing L'Enfant, designer of the city, seldom realizes that the Major of Engineers was not sacrificing convenience to looks in planning all those circles with spokelike thoroughfares radiating from them. The reason for them is that a single gun, planted in one of those circles, could sweep any of half a dozen avenues with grape-shot. Washington city was so planned that the government, with one regiment of artillery, could hold it against the most furious uprising of the slum population.

But by the end of ten years in Philadelphia, the government's tradition of dignity and firmness had been so well established by Washington and Adams that L'Enfant's precautions proved to be needless. No doubt they would have accomplished the same work anywhere, for they were great men; but no doubt they were helped by the fact that in those critical early years the capital was in a city in which the mob had little chance to make headway.

This is not an assertion that the Philadelphians of those years were virtuous and wise beyond the inhabitants of any other city. It is merely an assertion that they were cosmopolitan. Lying between the North and the South, lying between the wilderness and the sea, Philadelphia attracted representatives of every element of the American population—some of them very tough representatives; but the mixture made for quiet. If a demagogue raised a mob with one slogan, another demagogue could always raise a counter-mob with another slogan; and if one mob assailed the government, the other was certain to support it. It was so patently impossible, in such a town, for any one group of rioters to seize control that it was not seriously attempted; and the architects of the nation did their work in peace.

So did the carpenters, brickmasons, painters, and plasterers—that is to say, the little people whose names never appear in the annals of the republic but whose hands actually fastened it together. If the architects were such national heroes as Washington and Adams and such local heroes as bustling Dr. Benjamin Rush and cautious John Dickinson, the workmen were the anonymous twenty-eight thousand who filled the city.

It is all too easy for historians to ignore these, because their documentary records are scanty and rarely informative. Besides, when you have taken the trouble to isolate one, his contribution to the whole achievement is so small as to be imperceptible.

Nevertheless, the thousands took part in the extremely difficult work of fitting an old civilization to a new environment. This process had been going on since 1607, it is true, but after the political ties with Great Britain were severed, the emphasis shifted. For two hundred years it had been a resolute endeavor to make America English; but beginning with Independence Day, it was transformed into an effort to make English—the language, the people, and the culture—American.

Nobody sat down and wrote out the problem in such terms, of course, but the work went on, regardless of definitions. It went on everywhere, but for the ten years during which Philadelphia was the political, commercial, and intellectual capital, the movement centered there.

Respect for learning and the arts had, of course, been brought to America with the very first settlers. Captain John Smith, swashbuckler and hardfisted governor as he was, also was a man of letters, with five books to his credit, all of them popular successes, and all first-rate propaganda, if nothing more. The New Englanders had an immense regard for schooling, while the Calverts, in Maryland, and the Penns, in Pennsylvania, were aristocrats who expected the upper classes in their colonies to maintain the standards of English gentlemen.

But the colonists were content to try to transplant the arts and sciences. It was in Philadelphia, right after the consolidation of the colonies into a nation, that the attempt to naturalize them began in earnest. Its central location and commercial importance were not the only advantages the town possessed for the task. Two Benjamins had brought it into close working contact, one with English science, the other with English art. They were Benjamin Franklin, with his American Philosophical Society, and Benjamin West, with his school for young American artists in London.

For many years it was the fashion among American writers to speak of West a bit sniffishly. The sometime sign painter of Strawberry Alley never developed into a great artist, it is true, but he did become a very fine craftsman. More than that, the superpatriots who accuse him of running out on his country because he went to England and became Historical Painter to the King and his personal friend, are on doubtful ground. It can be argued just as plausibly that his country ran out on West, because he left five years before passage of the Stamp Act started the trouble; and before he was ready to return there was no longer a colony of Pennsylvania.

In any event, for fifty years the man was the friend—and a very powerful friend—of every young American who turned up in London, helping them financially, giving them valuable introductions, and teaching them in astonishing numbers. While Philadelphia was the national capital, Gil-

THE BUTCHER PARADE, A CEREMONY
THE ORIGINS OF WHICH ARE SECRETED
IN THE DARK RECESSES OF HISTORY

bert Stuart, John Trumbull, Thomas Sully, Charles Willson Peale, and Matthew Pratt, all pupils of West, were working there.

But it was a third Philadelphia Benjamin who exerted perhaps the most lasting effect on the development of American taste. This was Benjamin H. Latrobe, the architect, and the first great leader of what is known as the Greek Revival. His work, continued by that of his pupil William Strickland, dominated American architecture for fifty years. Latrobe's Bank of Pennsylvania was the first, and Strickland's Bank of the United States perhaps the most perfect, example of this style, which has the curious distinction of having dominated the imagination of Thomas Jefferson; for when he was an old man Jefferson abandoned the Palladian, which he had followed at Monticello, in favor of the Greek Revival, the style of the University of Virginia.

AT MAYOR POWEL'S
IN THE EVENING—RELAXATION
IN A HIGHLY CIVILIZED CITY

Latrobe was so powerful a personality that he probably could have imposed any style that struck his fancy upon his own city, at least to some extent. If he had gone Byzantine or Moorish, Philadelphia today might be full of turnip-shaped domes or spirally fluted columns. But, although a genius, he was still a man of his time, and his time was devoted to the neoclassic, predominantly Roman in Europe, especially in Napoleonic France, but so decidedly Greek in this country that the American name for the movement is not "neoclassicism," but "Greek Revival."

The reason stands out prominently. The republic was new, untried, uncertain, so men's minds inevitably sought any historical precedents that might guide them. The most brilliant examples of democracy in action were, of course, the Greek city-states, so Greek life was studied with avidity. Probably Philadelphia knew more about ancient Greece at this period than it has ever known before or since. Such men as Jefferson and John Adams habitually quoted Aristotle in the original; but at this time every lawyer defending a chicken thief in the inferior courts could cite—and be readily understood—arguments, not merely of Plato and Socrates, but of such smaller fry as Nicias, Aeschines, and Thrasybulus, as well.

It was the dawn calling to the dawn; and however often it ran into absurdity, there was in it a freshness, an energy, a sense of growing light that must be taken into account if one wishes to understand the conditions under which American liberty was nursed from infancy into vigorous maturity.

Music, in the America of 1800, was less of an art than an accomplishment, but it was not yet as strictly feminine an accomplishment as it became fifty years later. When Philadelphia was the capital, every gentleman aspired to take part in the musical ensembles that were a prominent phase of social life. As grave a philosopher and statesman as Jefferson regarded it as a misfortune of the most serious kind when a broken wrist, incompetently set, made it impossible for him to continue to play the violin; and at any party including more than half a dozen people, it was usual to find enough performers to play chamber music.

But the professionals were beginning to come in. For the most part, they were itinerants, following with curious fidelity a beaten path along the Atlantic Coast. A large proportion of them landed at Charleston and after a stay there, varying from a few days to a few years, moved to Norfolk, to Baltimore, to Philadelphia, to New York, to Boston, to Portland, Maine, and back again.

James Hewitt, Catherine Graupner, and the vast and formidable Dr. George K. Jackson were among the celebrities who tarried more or less briefly in Philadelphia in this period, but the town's own favorite was Mrs. Oldmixon, a soprano good enough, or who had been good enough, to enter into serious competition with the famous Mrs. Billington in London. Whether she was driven out of England by Billington's triumph, or by a tempestuous marriage with Sir John Oldmixon, a celebrated man about town, she came to America, had a long and brilliant career on the concert stage from Charleston to Portland, but eventually settled in Philadelphia, where she ended as mistress of an exclusive school for young ladies.

But the flat truth is that the arts, when Philadelphia was the capital of the United States, were embryonic in the whole country. An exception may be made of architecture, usually the first of the fine arts to be developed in a new country, because it is the most utilitarian of them all. The remotest frontier has to have housing, and constant demand for their services develops ability in the building trades that eventually flowers into art. The grace and the dignity of the best old Philadelphia buildings have rarely been equaled, and never surpassed, in later, larger, and costlier structures.

For the most part, however, the town in these years was laying the economic foundation that must underlie any considerable development of the aesthetic. Yet there was one product of her craftsmen that was rapidly approaching perfection, as far as beauty of design is concerned. This was the sailing ship, built, indeed, with the emphasis all on utility, but becoming more and more satisfying to the eye as its functional efficiency increased.

The clippers, the most beautiful of all sailing ships, were to come a little later, their development forced, first by the Napoleonic wars and then by the War of 1812. But Philadelphia was already turning out sturdy merchantmen, somewhat bluff-bowed as yet, but with an increasing sleekness of line in both hull and rig that was a prophecy of the grace and the speed that were not far ahead.

This industry had much to do with keeping Philadelphia always aware both of the wilderness behind her and of the great world to which the Delaware River was her broad avenue. From the forests, the farms, the little charcoal furnaces pushing deeper and deeper into the continent came the timber, the pitch, the hemp, the ironwork to make ships fit to battle their way around the Horn or Cape Comorin. And the ships coming back up the river were like the navy of Tarshish, "bringing gold and silver, ivory, and apes, and peacocks," but also bringing cargoes of which Solomon's navy never dreamed, English woolens, French wines and silks, Spanish velvets, Dominican mahogany, East Indian spices, Chinese porcelain, more valuable by far than the luxuries Solomon treasured, although ivory and apes and peacocks, too, have actually been landed at Philadelphia.

Naturally, it was not Philadelphia ships only that came up the broad avenue. All the maritime nations of the world were represented. All flags were to be seen along what later became Delaware Avenue, and this extreme eastern edge of Philadelphia was the extreme western edge of the Old World, equally, with Cadiz, or Marseilles, or Bombay, familiar with

> *Spanish sailors with bearded lips,*
> *And the beauty and mystery of the ships,*
> *And the magic of the sea.*

This contact with the Old World was important in the adolescent days of the New, for it was almost the only contact. Philadelphia itself, except along the water front, remained strikingly homogeneous. A strong German element had come in before the Revolution, and there were some remnants of the Swedish settlement a few miles down the Delaware, but the town as a whole, like the country behind it, remained predominantly English.

This is a factor frequently ignored by writers on the early history of the republic, but it must have had a strong influence on later developments. From 1789, the date of the outbreak of the French Revolution, until 1815, the end of the Napoleonic cycle, there was practically no emigration from Europe. For all those years Europe was hard put to it for manpower, and few were permitted to leave, even if they wished to do so. Yet between the census of 1790 and that of 1810, the population of the United States increased by 85 per cent, and by the end of another ten years it was two and

AT THE FOOT OF MARKET STREET
THE FRUITS OF ALL THE EARTH
WERE COLLECTED FOR PHILADELPHIANS

a half times what it had been in 1790. The first careful statistics of immigration date from 1820, the number in that year running to eight thousand; undoubtedly the average had been smaller, not larger, in the previous thirty years, yet there were five and a half million more persons in the country, and at eight thousand a year for thirty years only a quarter of a million could have come from abroad. The others were necessarily native products.

These figures are not to be taken too literally, for there was undoubtedly a larger factor of error in census taking in the early days; but after allowing for the largest margin of error that is within reason, certain inferences are not merely admissible, they are inevitable. One is that the racial type of the population did not change much during the first third of a century of the republic's existence; it remained predominantly English, or at least British. A second is that

CHESTNUT STREET'S NEW THEATER,
IN THE PERIOD WHEN ALL PHILADELPHIA
WAS NEW IN A NEW NATION

the early settlers were tremendously fecund, for it must not be forgotten that both infant and maternal mortality rates were, by modern standards, appallingly high. A third is that since life expectancy then was much lower than it is now, the proportion of old people in the total population must have been smaller.

All told, it is clear that in 1800, when the capital was removed to Washington, the number of Americans under twenty years of age in proportion to the whole population must have been enormously high. In Philadelphia it may have been somewhat lower because, like every other metropolis, it drew in from the surrounding country large numbers of workmen who had attained their majority and came to the city to practice their trades. But at that, it must have been a strikingly youthful population.

From the standpoint of the individual, this had its grim aspects. In the latter part of the eighteenth century, a Philadelphian's chances of surviving his first year were bad and his chances of surviving his fiftieth year even worse. But from the standpoint of the city, it made for vigor, confidence and boldness, not merely in politics but in every phase of life, notably in business.

They took hair-raising risks in those days, and frequently came to grief; but they won often enough to keep the majority encouraged. Robert Morris, the great financier of the Revolution, had carried through financial transactions that would appall a modern banker, but a combination of skill and luck enabled him to succeed. In the end, of course, he proved to be too bold, and he was no longer a young man, either. He was in his sixties when he acquired a tremendous acreage of wilderness in western New York and a large part of what is now the city of Washington; he borrowed to carry the deal, and it was too much for him. Taxes and interest were more than he could meet, and he crashed.

Yet his basic error was not lack of business acumen but lack of a crystal ball in which to read the future. He couldn't foresee Napoleon. He had counted on a flood of immigration, which eventually came, but too late for Morris. Napoleon had kept Europe in turmoil for twenty years, preventing any considerable flow of population to the New World, and the extraordinary fertility of his fellow citizens was of no avail, for Morris couldn't use babies to settle his lands.

The one phase of life in which Philadelphia was notably conservative—led in that direction by this same Morris—was finance. True, in this connection "conservative" is a relative term. The Bank of Pennsylvania, the Bank of North America, and, eventually, the First and Second banks of the United States were conservative only by comparison with the wildly reckless practices of nearly all other financial institutions.

But they established a tradition that has continued in Philadelphia ever since, to find expression in the twentieth century in the group of vast financial institutions, banks, insurance companies, trust companies, investment houses, that are the backbone of the city's wealth and power today.

Nicholas Biddle was a boy of fourteen when the capital

was removed to Washington, and his spectacular duel with the government itself for the control of American finance was still thirty years in the future; but already boldness and resolution, checked only by respect for sound business practice, were traditional among Philadelphia bankers.

In the perspective of a century and a half, the boldness and resolution are more conspicuous than the respect for precedent, and the moneyed men of the time have been held in low esteem. This is due in part to our forgetfulness of the role they played as builders. These early financiers were not exclusively manipulators of paper: many of them were driving forces in large construction projects.

True, the great works, especially the canals and the railroads, were to come later. But even at this time, at least two dreamers had found in Philadelphia substantial backing for the conversion of their dreams into reality. These were Oliver Evans, with his high-pressure steam engine, and John Fitch, with his steamboat. Evans patented a "steam wagon" in 1787, but did little with it; his more important work was in improving the stationary engine, which brought him the title "the Watt of America." Fitch, however, actually built and operated steamboats on the Delaware River long years ahead of Fulton on the Hudson.

Yet, although the Philadelphia bankers were excellent judges of men, they were not infallible. Just at the end of the period, in 1799, one of the few immigrants of the period arrived, came to Philadelphia and tried to purchase a powder factory at Frankford, but was unsuccessful, so he moved twenty miles down the river and bought a site near Wilmington, Delaware. On this occasion, the astute Philadelphians missed a bet. If they were interested in the commercial development of their city, they should have taken in that stranger, for his name was Éleuthère-Irénée Du Pont de Nemours, founder of the vast industrial empire now known as Dupont.

In general, however, it is true that Philadelphia, between Yorktown and the end of the century, did enjoy the distinction of being the market to which a young man with ideas should take them. If he had money, too, so much the better, but the town was definitely less interested in a man's cash than in his ability to think; so it became a magnet for talent, great and small.

This is well illustrated by the way it attracted such characters as brilliant, erratic, splenetic, and somewhat absurd Gouverneur Morris. This young man had already made a successful beginning at the bar in New York when he was elected to the Continental Congress in 1778; and when a coalition of his New York enemies defeated him for re-election, he found himself, like many a lame-duck member of Congress in the twentieth century, unable to tear himself away from the capital. He settled down to practice law, but was soon drawn back into the public service as an assistant to Robert Morris. This carried no taint of nepotism, for if the families were related at all, it was in England, several generations earlier. Gouverneur Morris was employed by Robert not as a kinsman but as an able financier, first in the government service, then as a business associate when both had returned to private life. Altogether, he remained in Philadelphia nearly ten years, and without doubt enjoyed life better there than in any other American city.

After Franklin, Gouverneur Morris was perhaps better attuned to the spirit of the town than any other of the Founding Fathers. He was very definitely one of them, for he served as a Pennsylvania delegate to the Constitutional Convention and took a leading part in the debates, speaking more often, perhaps, than any other. He belonged to the Hamiltonian school of thought and found the finished work very much too democratic for his taste, but supported its ratification; so he was as certainly a Founding Father as Madison, "father of the Constitution."

But he was a Father with a difference, and it may be argued plausibly that the difference was that, regardless of

GENERAL WASHINGTON CALLS
ON MISTRESS BETSY ROSS TO THANK
HER FOR THE FLAG HE DEFENDED

Saint Margarets School

Waterbury, Connecticut

his birth in New York, he was temperamentally more truly Philadelphian than Washington, Jefferson, Hamilton, or Madison. For this gentleman thought it important to be amused. He was a fighter of undeniable prowess, who enjoyed a good fight. But he enjoyed the pleasures of the town, also, and took pains to cultivate them. He enjoyed the ludicrousness of things in general, and especially of some of his sterner colleagues, and he saw no reason to disguise his enjoyment, so he collected enemies right and left. In a runaway, he was thrown from his carriage, and a leg was shattered so badly that it had to be amputated; but even stumping along on a wooden peg he continued to be amused.

In all this he matched the spirit of the town. Philadelphia thought it worth while to be amused. The vast historical significance of the events occurring there has obscured this fact, but a fact it was. No doubt President Washington sat

THIS GUNBOAT BELONGED TO THE PENNSYLVANIA NAVY, OLDER THAN THAT OF THE UNITED STATES with bowed head and furrowed brow, bending under the burdens of his office. No doubt Mr. Jefferson and Mr. Hamilton glared at each other across the Cabinet table, each darkly suspecting the other of plotting to overthrow the American government by force and violence. No doubt members of Congress discharged orations into the quivering air of what had been Carpenters', but was now Congress Hall, with a passionate solemnity capable of really believing that they were overshadowing Demosthenes. No doubt the great were weighed down by the perplexities and the responsibilities attached to the creation of a new nation. But Philadelphia and Mr. Morris enjoyed life; and their enjoyment probably exerted a definite, if unsuspected, influence toward making our governmental institutions more reasonable, more human.

Of course, there is an argument to be made in support of the theory that it is inadmissible to cite Gouverneur Morris as typifying early Philadelphia, when Dr. Benjamin Rush is available. The argument is seductive, because Rush was not only a native of the town but a much more attractive character. Morris was basically sour, and later in life he became the envenomed foe of democracy, while Rush, in spite of his resounding battles with his own profession, was essentially sweet-spirited.

But the argument is unsound because Rush was a wild enthusiast, and this was flatly, definitely, finally not Philadelphian. He was amusingly well named, for he took after every idea that crossed his mind like an ill-trained bird dog after rabbits. He was successively Presbyterian, Episcopalian, Universalist, and Unitarian; furthermore, he listened with avidity to George Whitefield in this country, and to the Scottish philosophers at Edinburgh, leading to the suspicion that he may have been a Methodist and a Deist also. He was an essayist, a penologist, an abolitionist, a feminist, a psychiatrist, and a phlebotomist, this last-named enthusiasm leading William Cobbett to observe that the doctor's practice of bleeding was "one of the great discoveries . . . which have contributed to the depopulation of the earth." He signed the Declaration of Independence, demanded that Washington be relieved of his command, fought for the adoption of the Constitution, and is said to have instructed three thousand American physicians.

A man who rushed into everything was certainly not a typical Philadelphian of the period. He was a curiosity—an ornament, too, no doubt—and perhaps in some degree the city's joy and pride, but not its true representative. Yet toward the end of his tremendous life, Benjamin Rush did one thing that was Philadelphian in its very essence. He was the mediator who composed the long quarrel between John Adams and Thomas Jefferson, so bringing about the correspondence between the two old statesmen that stands to this day as one of the finest monuments of the influence of the humanities on the American mind. Philadelphia was certainly the reconciler of differences in those days, the meeting place of honest but opposing minds; so in this instance, Rush was typical, after all.

Perhaps he may be called truly Philadelphian also in the

broad range of his interests. His studies of yellow fever were strictly professional, and his crusade against alcoholism was within his field as a physician. But he also inquired into the limits of sovereignty of the British crown, into the reform of correctional institutions, into the system of education of young women, into the possibility of abolishing both pauperism and chattel slavery, which are hardly to be described as medical problems. Furthermore, he wrote in a popular style that established him as a man of letters, the first American physician to be so recognized.

Finally, it may be claimed that he qualified as a true Philadelphian by attaining a distinguished position as an ancestor. Two of his sons, James, physician and psychologist, and Richard, lawyer and diplomatist, kept the name illustrious for half a century after the old doctor was laid in the Christ Church graveyard; which may be pure chance, but is a thing to which Philadelphia has always ascribed merit.

Incidentally, Dr. Benjamin Rush had a cousin, William

Rush, whose career is an illuminating commentary not so much on Philadelphia as on the country as a whole. He is remembered today as the founder, with Charles Willson Peale, of the Pennsylvania Academy of Fine Arts, the first organization of its kind in America and one that has had an exceptionally distinguished history. This event came in 1805, a little after the period under discussion, but Rush and Peale were both active in Philadelphia while it was the national capital.

They were both artists, Peale a painter, Rush a sculptor, and both men with a definite native talent. But in a raw, new country, development of talent of that kind was difficult to the point of impossibility. To begin with, in their early youth, when it would have been most effective, competent instruction was almost entirely lacking. Peale, at twenty-six, did manage to get to London, where he studied under Benjamin West, but that was pretty late for the finest development of his talent, while Rush apparently never served under a real master. But worse than the lack of formal instruction was the lack of discriminating patronage that would enable them to live by their art.

They were put to odd expedients to keep body and soul together. Peale kept a museum that included many of his paintings, a live rattlesnake, and the bones of a mammoth; Rush spent the major part of his life carving figureheads for ships. Rarely, if ever, has a great art gallery had a more astonishing origin. Artists in early America had a rough time; their story leaves one divided between regret for the frustration and waste, and admiration of the resolution of men to develop "that one talent which is death to hide."

The whole American story is, of course, the story of the adaptation of an old civilization to new conditions for which it was not designed, and such an endeavor always involves some tragedy, as well as much ingenuity, courage, determination, and endurance. The fighting from 1776 to 1783, which we call the American Revolution, was only the political phase of a vastly greater operation that began in 1607 and is not completed yet—the imposition of Western European civilization upon another hemisphere. In North America, the spearhead was the British, in South America, the Spanish phase of that civilization; but in both continents, the whole culture necessarily underwent a profound transformation, one so profound that to European observers it seemed to mean the disappearance of culture altogether.

Yet while the transformation of the political organization was merely an episode, it was the most spectacular episode in the whole story. It brought clearly into men's minds realization that a change was taking place; and that gives it an interest and a significance attaching to no other. So Philadelphia, as the official center of the transfer from one political form to another, stands out as the showpiece of the whole thing. The lives and labors, the studies and the sports of its citizens—not merely the great men in Congress, or in

THE OLD LONDON COFFEE HOUSE,
WHICH WAS A STOCK EXCHANGE
LONG BEFORE THE REVOLUTIONARY WAR

the Federal, the state, and the municipal offices, but the ordinary burghers—carry a significance vastly greater than is apparent on the surface.

Take, for example, the butchers' celebration, which was, in its general tone of revelry, strikingly like the Mummers' parade of the next century. But it was more than that. It was almost the last manifestation of a social order that had once been all-powerful in Europe, the guild system. The guilds were, it is true, something like labor unions, but that statement should be accepted in the sense that one accepts the statement that the King was something like the President. The differences are more prominent than the similarities.

The guilds themselves were derived from more ancient organizations reaching so far back into history that they touched the point at which religion, economics, and politics could not be distinguished. The flower-bedecked steer

RICKETT'S CIRCUS, AT SIXTH
AND CHESTNUT, WHERE CHEERFUL
PHILADELPHIA MADE MERRY

that the Philadelphia butchers drove through the streets was the lineal descendant of the creature pictured on the Grecian urn that set John Keats to wondering—

To what green altar, O mysterious priest,
Lead'st thou that heifer lowing at the skies,
And all her silken flanks with garlands dressed?

The Philadelphia butchers would have laughed uproariously at the idea that they followed a "mysterious priest" to a religious ceremony, but the line of descent is clear.

The old customs, however, did not last. Even in the decade between 1790 and 1800, they were either dying out or being transformed into something more characteristic of the New World than of the Old. Up in New York, for instance, the Dutch, who got there first, had brought over the charming tradition of Sant Nikolaas, patron of childhood, and the English, coming later, brought Father Christmas. But the Americans combined the two into Santa Claus, who doesn't look quite right to either Dutch or English.

This transformation of ways of thinking, acting, and even feeling from the forms accepted for centuries in Europe to new forms adapted to this country is hard to trace, historically, but it is a highly important part of the American story. The popular theory that attributes it all to the influx of non-English-speaking immigrants does not stand up under examination, for the change began long before other nationalities began to arrive in force. George Washington was not an English country gentleman, although he was much like one, and, when he was President, Philadelphia was not an English market town, although it was much like one. The changes were so small that they are hard to describe, but the changes were more significant than the survivals, because the changes indicated the direction in which the development of the country was to proceed.

It was not that the Americans had developed a reasonless hatred of the old ways or cherished any conscious desire to change them; it was simply that the new environment imposed new ways. Philadelphia merchants, for example, dealt with farmers whose problems were not those of the farmers who came to the English market towns. The first problem of the American farmer was usually that of clearing heavily timbered land, something that had been done for the Englishman generations before his time.

The American, therefore, having to begin as a lumberman, needed implements that the English farmer never heard of—the peavey, for example, had to be invented here. The Englishman had not even curved the handle of his ax, and because he used it relatively infrequently, his interest in the quality of the bit was less; but the American, forced to practice constantly, became expert in the use of the ax and fastidious as to the temper, the weight, and the balance of the tool. The plow that was well adapted to turning English soil that had been cultivated for centuries was all but useless on newly cleared land full of stumps and roots. One of Jefferson's chief triumphs as an inventor was a moldboard, still in use.

The Philadelphia merchant, therefore, had to supply

equipment that an English merchant never saw, which meant that he had to solve problems not presented to his confrere. The so-called "Kentucky rifle" was a product of Pennsylvania, an illustration of the way American business modified the methods brought from England to serve the needs of the frontier. The businessman, although he may never suspect it, is inevitably shaped and molded by his customers; to meet their requirements, he must understand their problems; to understand their problems, he must think their thoughts; and in thinking their thoughts, he becomes to some extent one of them. So Philadelphia, although it was molded on an English town, was never an English town, not even in the years before any considerable number of non-English newcomers had invaded it.

What was true of the merchants applied with equal force to other townsmen. English doctors, for instance, rarely, if ever, had to cope with epidemics of yellow fever, or with malaria, or with the "milk sickness" that a generation later orphaned Abraham Lincoln; or with the stresses that the violent American climate puts upon body and mind. Braddock proved that the European art of war was worthless in the forest against savages. Even the theologians found sin breaking out in unfamiliar forms and had to shift their own ground to combat Satan effectively.

As for the lawyers, once the political separation was effected their professional attitudes had to be reconstructed from the ground up. Nor were the crafts unaffected: carpentry and masonry had to take into account the effects of temperatures more extreme than those of England; joiners and cabinetmakers had to adjust their work to an abundance of wood and a scarcity of nails; while cookery, coping with new materials, was radically modified.

The fact was that Philadelphia, like every other town in the New World, could not, rather than would not, be English. This is so obvious today that merely to restate it seems a dismal threshing of old straw; yet it was so incredible to mercantilist England that it was the wedge that split the empire. To eighteenth-century England, an English colony was merely a group of transplanted Englishmen, owing the same allegiance to England that they owed at home. Even in the eighteenth century, rational Englishmen would not have expected the inhabitants of Cadiz to act like Englishmen; but it was beyond their capacity to believe that the inhabitants of Philadelphia were in important respects, as foreign as Spaniards. So the London government proceeded to exact of the Americans a degree of subservience that no self-respecting people, conscious of their own identity as a people, could accept; and presently the Continental Congress was assembled in Philadelphia with Colonel Washington, delegate from Virginia, in full uniform; then, after a dozen years, the Constitutional Convention met in the same room, with General Washington presiding; and finally, the Congress of the United States sat in Carpenters' Hall, listening to the messages of President Washington.

A thousand factors contributed to bring about this series of events, but the basic one was the failure to realize that a difference did exist between Englishmen and Americans and that the law must allow for this difference. This failure was not confined entirely to London; it was three-quarters of a century before Americans themselves got around to writing in the supreme law of the land that "all persons born or naturalized in the United States and subject to the jurisdiction thereof, are citizens of the United States and of the State wherein they reside."

This reluctance to admit that birth or residence in America affected the status of Englishmen was due to traditional English jealous preservation of the rights of Englishmen, a jealousy as powerful in Philadelphia as in London. Any admission that any difference existed would have broken the force of the colonists' contention that, as Englishmen, they were entitled to representation in the English legislature; so not until the political ties with

ONE OF THE NATION'S SHRINES,
WHERE THE CONTINENTAL CONGRESS MET,
NOW CALLED CONGRESS HALL

Britain were severed could Americans consistently insist upon their separate nationality; and not until the Constitution went into effect did "We, the people of the United States" begin to function as a nation in fact as well as in name.

So it was in Philadelphia that Americanism was not, indeed, born, for it was born when the first permanent settler took up residence on the continent, but nursed into conscious life. This was the rising sun that Franklin saw, although he would have been hard put to it to describe it.

But before a modern American sneers at Franklin on that account let him try to describe it himself. It is easy to point out where our political institutions and laws differ from those of Great Britain, but institutions and laws are the product, not the producer, of national spirit—"nationalism" is the word, but of late nationalism has come to mean

JAMES WILSON, LAWYER
ABOUT TO SPEAK TO AN AUDIENCE
IN THE FIRST AMERICAN LAW SCHOOL

strutting belligerence, and so is spoiled for its proper use.

Most certainly the Americanism that was developed at Philadelphia while the government resided there was not comprised in the acts of that government. They influenced it profoundly, of course, but they did not create it and they did not control it. On the other hand, it was not a Philadelphia municipal project, either. Every visitor from other parts of the country influenced it, and influenced Philadelphia too. The town became different and remained different because of the presence there of such men as Mr. Adams, of Massachusetts, Mr. Jefferson, of Virginia, Mr. Hamilton, of New York, and the Messrs. Pinckney, of South Carolina. It was also affected by the presence there of Mennonite farmers, of Dutch sailors, of Negro slaves, of Maryland tobacco growers, of frontier fur trappers, of some specimen of practically every human variety to be found in the United States. Obscure men, as well as famous ones, counted.

But if these affected Philadelphia, as they assuredly did,

it is a reasonable assumption that Philadelphia, in turn, affected them. In those critical years when the new government was first taking definite form, the environment in which the work was done had an effect, insensible, perhaps, but definite, on that work. The United States of today is what it is in part—perhaps in larger part than we usually imagine—because its structure was first put together in a city that was youthful, vigorous, confident, and cheerful.

It may be that there are some reasons for regretting this. It is at least arguable that, had they worked in an older town, the framers of the government might have avoided some errors that resulted from youthful inexperience. For example, in a city as old as, say, Amsterdam, Mr. Hamilton might have found it far easier to erect a sensible fiscal structure, might, in fact, have erected a better one. In such an environment, General Knox would certainly have had a better chance to maintain an adequate military establishment, and Mr. Jefferson might have created the national university of which he dreamed.

But these possible advantages would have been obtained at the price of certain very definite losses. It is impossible to believe that the architects of the government, working in the atmosphere of a capital as old as London, or Paris, or Vienna, would have dared exhibit such sublime faith in the capacity of the people to govern themselves. At this very moment, indeed, Edmund Burke in London was proclaiming, "Better to be despised for too anxious apprehensions, than ruined by too confident a security," and his definition of "too confident a security" was the theory that the people have a right, first, to choose their own governors, second, to cashier them for misconduct, and, third, to frame a government for themselves—precisely the principles on which the Americans were working.

None but a cheerfully confident people could possibly have carried to a successful issue the kind of work that was done in Philadelphia. They were trying it in Paris at that very moment; the French effort was the occasion for Burke's outburst. But the atmosphere of Paris was anything but cheerfully confident; on the contrary, it was as grimly determined as the Moscow of a century and a half later, and, as in Moscow, the effort was attended by frightful blood purges. Eventually, the French did erect a workable form of democracy, but not in ten years, or several times ten years.

On the other hand, Philadelphia was not a remote frontier outpost. Even Talleyrand found it endurable—not to his taste, to be sure, but still definitely a civilized city. When so highly sophisticated a European could stand it at any price, it is safe to say that the men who fabricated the United States government were not working in a vacuum, cut off from all contact with the main current of ideas in Western civilization. On the contrary, every important member of their group was thoroughly conversant with the trend of European thought, and some of them had a better understanding of Europe than is exhibited by half of their modern successors.

Indeed, from the wildest part of the Pennsylvania wilderness, from the heart and center of the Whisky Rebellion, from the frontier itself, came one of the most highly cultivated of the early American leaders. In 1794, the country beyond the Alleghenies sent as its representative to the Congress in Philadelphia a man named Abraham Alfonse Albert Gallatin, whom Henry Adams, usually deemed an authority on education, if nothing else, called "perhaps the best-informed man in the country."

Gallatin knew Locke and Montesquieu, Grotius and Plato, for in his youth he had received as good an education as Switzerland, where he was born, could supply, which meant about as good as Europe could supply; but he also knew the frontier and the frontiersmen, for in his twenties he had carved out an estate on the banks of the Monongahela when that area was as complete a wilderness as one can imagine. Gallatin had not merely read the political philosophers, he had understood them; and he had not merely become acquainted with backwoodsmen, he understood them, too, so well that he was able to act as peacemaker between the distillers and the revenue officers at the time of the Whisky Rebellion.

To this knowledge of lawgivers and lawbreakers, he added another kind of knowledge, then rare in America. He knew the history of the Fuggers and the Medici, the creators of international banking; and when *The Wealth of Nations* appeared in 1776, he knew what Adam Smith was talking about better than half the businessmen in London. The chancelleries of Europe held few men with a broader and more comprehensive knowledge of the theories of government, from the Greeks down, and none who added to that knowledge gained from books, Gallatin's intimate understanding gained from experience, of how and what the masses of the people were thinking.

His great work was done years later, of course, when he was Secretary of the Treasury in Washington; but in Philadelphia, between 1795 and 1800, he rose to leadership of the opposition in the House of Representatives. The presence of even one such man in Congress was a sufficient guarantee that its debates would not sink to the level of a squabble among peasants; and Gallatin had both followers and opponents worthy of his steel.

This is not to be understood as an assertion that Philadelphia in these days was a new Athens. On the contrary, in its basic concept of organized society it was the exact opposite of Athens, for where Athens held that the individual is an implement of the state, Philadelphia held that the state is an implement of the individual.

But it did resemble, not the Athens of Pericles but the earlier city of Solon, in that in Philadelphia at this time more hard, original, and effective thinking about the nature of government was being done than in any other city in the world. Conventional thinkers may denounce the suggestion as preposterous, but look at the record. That people were

A VOLUNTEER FIRE COMPANY
FACES AN URBAN PROBLEM IN THE DAYS
WHEN AMERICA WAS NEARLY ALL RURAL

thinking hard will perhaps be granted, for they were in a jam, and knew it. The stupidest man, when he knows he is in a tight place, will think as hard as he is able; and so will the wisest man. Mental exertion was not confined to Congress, formerly Carpenters' Hall; it was going on everywhere —in the shops, in the taverns, in drawing rooms and market places; wherever Philadelphians and the crowds of strangers who thronged Philadelphia gathered, they were constantly talking about government, and those who could think were thinking about it.

It is doubtless true that this kind of thing contributed nothing measurable to political philosophy, but to dismiss it as of no importance whatever is going too far. At least it created an atmosphere favorable to the development of ideas, for the able men who were doing the important thinking were keenly aware that every suggestion they advanced

THE LIBRARY IN FIFTH STREET
WHEN PHILADELPHIA WAS INTRODUCING
THE AMENITIES OF LIFE

would be pounced upon, discussed, denounced, defended, and scrutinized by thousands of people. Rare, indeed, is the man who is not stimulated by daily and hourly evidence that what he is doing is regarded as important by thousands of people, even people whose own mental capacity is not impressive.

That the thinking was original is evidenced by the fact that to this day it has not been completely understood, even by Americans, to say nothing of foreigners. An entirely satisfactory definition, not of Americanism, which is by its very nature a vague concept, but of the American theory of government, which would seem to be a much more concrete thing, is still lacking after a hundred and forty years. Consider, for example, Hamilton's famous *Report on Manufactures,* written in Philadelphia and presented to Congress in the winter of 1791–1792. Hamilton was a master of lucid English, and any schoolboy can understand the language of that report without turning to a dictionary; but some of the shrewdest minds in the country have battled over its implications without ever reaching final and complete agreement.

Philadelphia, indeed, had little chance of understanding fully what was going on because frantic efforts were made to keep it in a state of confusion by the three great journalists of the period: Bache, Freneau, and Fenno. Benjamin Franklin Bache, a native product, was a grandson of the philosopher, although anything but a philosopher himself, and the original mouthpiece of the Jeffersonians. To combat him, the Hamiltonians imported John Fenno from New York, and when Bache became rather too virulent to be effective the Jeffersonians brought in Philip Freneau, also from New York. Personal abuse and vilification were the chief weapons employed by all three, which meant, of course, that the real truth was almost entirely concealed from the readers of the papers. They did, however, have the merit of keeping interest in the affairs of government extremely alive and alert.

Yet if all three editors had exhibited the calm reasonableness of Socrates before his judges, it is hardly to be supposed that they could have enlightened the city to any great extent. For what was being done was definitely new in the history of government, and pathfinding is by its very nature perplexing and obscure. It was so then; it is so now; it was so in the Athens of Solon. The thinking of Europe between 1790 and 1800 was divided between the theory that the Americans were, in Samuel Johnson's words, "a race of convicts," and the theory that they might be honest but were definitely insane—a division that seems to be fairly prevalent in Europe to this day. To this extent, at least, our early capital was truly Athenian, for just so the surrounding nations thought of Athens when it was struggling to formulate its political theory.

Finally, the thinking that was done in Philadelphia when it was the capital was effective. The proof is the results. The government that took shape in those critical years has its faults and weaknesses, to be sure, and is a long way from the perfection dreamed of by Plato, but it certainly is not a failure. It has ridden out the storms of a century and a half and at this moment is dominant in half the world.

John Locke devised for the two Carolinas the form and framework of a government theoretically more perfect than our union, and James Oglethorpe made one for Georgia at least as good. But both were stillborn; they never even kicked. They were long ago forgotten and do not appear in any list of states that have fallen. The vital spark was not in them—so they were not, in fact, governments.

The most dismal pessimist cannot deny that there was life in what men made in Philadelphia. In the middle of the twentieth century, our most outspoken detractors, the Russians, are asserting that there was all too much life in it, that it was a new, a subtler, and therefore a more dangerous imperialism. Some of our own left wing, while not going that far, have seen in it an effort to repeal by amendment the Declaration of Independence; but they do not suggest that it was lifeless.

Life, however, is indescribable. We can perceive and define its manifestations, but the thing itself eludes us. Perhaps the time will come when some philosopher will be able to capture Americanism and imprison it in words, but not until this republic is as dead as Elizabethan England. We can analyze republican Rome cleverly and plausibly, but only because it is dead, desiccated, and extant only as a laboratory specimen; we can also analyze our own republic and account very exactly for everything about it except what makes it go; but when we except that, we except the conclusion of the whole matter.

So it would be arrant folly to attempt to state why the thinking done in Philadelphia at this time was effective. Certain men in a certain environment under certain circumstances evolved certain political ideas, and they worked. So much we know, but all the rest is guessing; yet it is good guessing to say that if you omit from your calculation anything, even what seems to be the least important factor, you may be omitting the very thing that could lead you to the truth.

We can see a connection between the fact that they read European philosophers in Philadelphia and the fact that the framework of the new government proved to be intellectually sound. But the fact that they gave good dinners in Philadelphia, and built good ships in Philadelphia, and drove a thriving trade in Philadelphia may seem to have no bearing on the matter. Yet the builders of the nation, being human, must have been affected by their environment; they worked in an environment in which great things were in preparation, and they prepared a great thing. It is hard to believe that this is wholly without significance.

For Philadelphia in these years was laying the groundwork for the achievements of the nineteenth century. The Schuylkill Canal, first of a long series of great public works, was not opened until 1824, and industry, in the form of the factory system rather than handicrafts, got its first great impetus at the time of the War of 1812, but the spirit of enterprise, the imagination, and the daring requisite to undertake such tremendous projects were being developed while the seat of the national government was located in the town.

Certainly this atmosphere was no handicap, and it was probably a definite stimulus, to the men who were undertaking a political enterprise more gigantic by far than all that Philadelphia accomplished or dreamed of accomplishing. They might have worked as well elsewhere, but the facts of human nature give one leave to doubt it.

The resilience of the American political system accounts for its survival for a longer period than any other democracy of comparable size; and it is resilient because the men who wrote the Constitution, and those who guided the nation through its first difficult years were too conscious of their own imperfections to cast the system into a rigid logical mold. They had followed Cromwell's advice to the Scotch Presbyterians—they had allowed God to show them that it

THE FRIGATE "PHILADELPHIA"
BEING BUILT FOR THE FLEDGLING NAVY
ABOUT THE YEAR 1800

was possible for them to be mistaken—and in all their work they made some allowance for the factor of error.

No doubt George Washington was chiefly responsible for this, first through his own wise leadership, but also through a policy, for which he has been criticized, of including disparate elements in the first Cabinet. This led to clashes, it is true, but it also had the important effect of making it impossible for either Mr. Hamilton or Mr. Jefferson to become too certain of the perfection of his own ideas. When an alert and powerful mind is ready with instant criticism of everything one does, one is unlikely to develop delusions of omniscience. In the formative years, it was even more important than it has been since for our leaders to realize that they were not all-wise.

Yet while the chief credit must be given to Washington, surely something must be accorded to Philadelphia. From

WHEN EVERY GENTLEMAN WAS
A MAN-AT-ARMS—FENCING
AT M. DE FLORETTE'S ACADEMY

its earliest days, Penn's town had acknowledged the necessity of a policy of give-and-take in the relations of men. Penn's government had been strongly moralistic, but not theocratic; in England the Quakers had been a barely tolerated sect, and in America they knew that enjoyment of their own rights was contingent upon their recognizing the rights of others. The experience of a hundred years had shown that religious toleration was not only necessary but highly successful—Maryland and Pennsylvania, two centers of religious freedom, were more consistently profitable to their proprietors than any of the other colonies.

So when Mr. Hamilton and Mr. Jefferson took that extremely important walk down the street in the course of which Mr. Jefferson agreed to support assumption of the state debts and Mr. Hamilton agreed to support the location of the capital on the banks of the Potomac, they were definitely acting in the Philadelphian spirit. The air would have been less conducive to compromise had they been walking through Boston, with its stern tradition of adherence to principle even though it meant the stake; or through Charleston, with its tradition of submission to the direction of a ruling class.

Mr. Jefferson later claimed that he consented to an injustice because he was bemused by Mr. Hamilton's eloquence, but historians have been loath to credit that. He must have known that he was allowing certain highly dubious characters to get away with worse than dubious profits on that deal; but he also knew that the act would strengthen and stabilize a union that desperately needed strength and stability. The future profit was vastly greater than the immediate loss, and it was certainly in accord with the reasonable spirit of Philadelphia to do what could be done, rather than hold out for the ideal at great risk of getting nothing.

If the atmosphere of the place, as much as Mr. Hamilton's argument, subtly influenced Mr. Jefferson's mind toward compromise, the country was definitely the gainer in the end. If the atmosphere of the place influenced Washington to make that great plea for reason in politics which is the

Farewell Address, and helped John Adams hold out for reason in foreign relations in 1798, when the hysterical were
demanding war with France, there can be no doubt that the
atmosphere of the place was a beneficent influence.

In any event, the most superficial examination of the record brings out one fact with great clarity. It is the fact that
the framework of this republic was put together by men who
were not only wise, brave, and resolute, but hopeful and, on
the whole, cheerful men. The deal between Hamilton and
Jefferson, for instance, could not have been made by pessi-
mists. Hamilton wished to saddle the infant nation with
what was, for the time, a colossal debt. By staving off immediate interest payments he admitted that the nation could
not at the time carry the load; but he was perfectly sure that
it would rapidly acquire strength to do so. Jefferson wished

WHEN PHILADELPHIA WAS
STILL ALL ENGLISH—A CRICKET
MATCH IN PRE-REVOLUTIONARY TIMES

to remove the capital out into the woods and fields, far from any great center of population, confident that very soon a sufficient community would grow up around it to afford the amenities of civilized life.

The curious thing is that both erred on the side of conservatism. Hamilton's debt was not only carried but was paid off almost twice as fast as he had expected. Jefferson's hundred square miles proved too small to contain the city that has grown up at the seat of government. In 1846 men who did not share Jefferson's vision returned to Virginia that part of the District of Columbia which it had ceded, and that, not the greatness of the original concept, was the error.

This is interesting, to say the least, at a time when the United States again is facing palpable dangers and problems to whose solution precedent furnishes no guide. As it was in

THE NATION'S CHILDHOOD
WAS NOT A SAD ONE—SKATERS
ON THE DELAWARE ABOUT 1784

the administrations of President Washington and President Adams, so now we have our element, including many good people, honest people, thoughtful people, who are appalled by the responsibilities that have been thrust upon us and by the risks that they entail. Their anxiety is not relieved when they observe the brisk confidence with which others insist on driving ahead; on the contrary, irritation is added to anxiety, and they are more unhappy than ever.

The worst of it is that nobody can reassure them, for nobody really knows what lies ahead. No other nation has preceded us down the path we are taking, and what lions may stand in the way, what robbers may be lurking around every bend in the road, we can find out only by venturing to the encounter. The state of the nation is by no means soothing even to the ordinarily prudent, and to the timorous these are truly dreadful days.

But this adds value to our memories of old Philadelphia, especially when we pay less attention to the solemnities of statecraft and more to the way the people actually lived in that place and that period. The contrast with modern Washington is rather striking. When Philadelphia was the political capital, it was full of gossip and scandalmongering; the newspapers of Bache, Fenno, and Freneau prove that beyond a doubt. Perhaps it was as full of irresponsible talk as modern Washington, although that is a strong statement. But Philadelphia did not live on its nerves. The overwhelming majority of the population were not government employees but were engaged in productive labor of some kind; and their enterprises were so varied that calamity to one line of business could not paralyze the town. If the wheat crop failed and the grist mills halted, shipping would keep things going; and if the ships and shipyards were idle, the tanneries and metalworking industries would help. Washington, on the contrary, is convulsed every fourth year, when the quadrennial crisis approaches in its sole industry, politics. In short, Philadelphia, between 1790 and 1800, was much more truly representative of the attitudes and emotions of the whole American people. It embodied a steadiness always to be found in the people, but not always apparent in modern Washington.

It was in that atmosphere that great work was done. It was the people who were briskly confident, not those who were wretchedly apprehensive, who were more nearly in the right; although, as the event proved, the confident were not confident enough, the optimistic were not as cheerful as history shows they had a right to be.

Whether there is significance in this for the modern world every man will decide for himself. If he is pessimistic by nature, he will doubtless argue that things are so different now that what occurred in Philadelphia a hundred and sixty years ago no longer has any meaning; but if he is a born optimist, he will take note that it was the bold, brisk fellows in a bold, brisk city who knew what they were about, and it

IN A PHILADELPHIA WHICH
SOME THOUGHT SCANDALOUSLY GAY,
RACERS PASS THE PRESIDENT'S HOUSE

was the calamity howlers who were utterly wrong; and he will argue that it may be so again, even if our modern difficulties are frightening in their size and obscurity.

In either case, however, it is well to know as much as we can of the conditions under which our political leaders worked when they were doing what turned out to be an extraordinarily good job. For nobody, or at least no good union man, will challenge the assertion that working conditions are bound to affect the job. It does not necessarily follow that if we could reproduce the conditions we could also reproduce the efficiency; but there is always the chance that we might.

The United States of America today is a colossal power, absolutely, as well as relatively, one of the strongest, in the material sense, that the world has ever seen. Hence, every circumstance relating to its origin and development is

A SPECIMEN OF THE WORK
OF AMERICA'S FIRST MINT IS EXAMINED
BY ITS DIRECTOR IN 1792

bound to be of interest to students of history, not in this country only but everywhere. In particular, any marked difference in the origin of this power and the origin of comparable powers elsewhere in the world deserves attention and study, for, although it may seem trivial, it might have an important bearing upon the art and the mystery of political organization.

One particular in which the United States is conspicuously different from all its predecessors as a world power is the fact that it was not created in some ancient, wealthy, and powerful city, overshadowing all the region tributary to it, some Susa, some Babylon, some Rome. The United States did not come out of a London, or a Paris, built by the slow accretions of centuries, and developing in the course of centuries formidable tribal chiefs who constituted, with their families, a nobility strongly entrenched and not to be displaced without terrific social convulsions.

The birthplace of the Revolution was Boston. The birthplace of the United States was Philadelphia, and although the exigencies of war forced the removal of its capital successively to Baltimore, to York, to Lancaster, to Annapolis, and to New York, they were all small towns and relatively new. Lancaster and York were place names, with no reference to the badge of the White Rose or the Red; Philadelphia had nothing remotely comparable to the names of Guise and Valois, or to the Roman Patricians, or the Spartan Heraclidae. Thus, the new nation emerged unscarred by the wars of strong and ambitious noblemen.

More than that, all the ancient cities had developed, alongside their wealth and magnificence, cesspools of human misery that appalled philosophers from the earliest times. The *faubourgs* of Paris were spewing up mobs that were wrecking France while Philadelphia was our capital, and ten years earlier Lord George Gordon had drawn from the slums of London an army of misery so appalling that it shook the British throne. As a result, every government in Europe lived in mortal terror of the mob. Even the government of the United States, after the mutiny of the Pennsylvania troops, had its moments of uneasiness, reflected in L'Enfant's plan of Washington, but the danger here was relatively remote, so the formidable safeguards against rioters, elsewhere considered essential although they limited freedom, were unnecessary here.

The United States, alone among the great powers, was started on its way in a neat, new, clean little town where differences in rank did not exist, and where differences in wealth were not conspicuously great. This meant that the men responsible for shaping the course of the new nation were relieved of a large group of problems that had harried and harassed men in a similar position elsewhere. Earlier revolutionaries had usually worked under a very real threat of sudden violent death, and always under the pressure of a mass of prejudices and traditions from which the Americans were happily free.

To say that this had no effect upon their course of action would be to say that they were different from all the rest of humanity. Fear and hatred are the great distorters of judg-

ment. They distorted the judgment of the Americans somewhat, causing them to omit from the Constitution a provi-
sion for the progressive elimination of slavery, and to insert
in it the unworkable idea of the electoral college to select
the President, to mention only two of the defects in their
scheme of government.

Yet the Americans were relatively free from influences
that make for unsound judgment because they worked in
such a town as Philadelphia then was—busy, intelligent, tolerant, and cheerful. Never believe that this had no influence
on the excellence of the work. Perhaps it had a much
stronger influence than we are accustomed to think; and certainly any serious student of our government ought to take
it into account.

For the value of the story of old Philadelphia is, above all
else, the conclusive proof it affords of a theory that had been
debated from the beginning of history, but never before
subjected to experimental test—the theory that men, given
a fair chance, can devise for themselves governmental insti-

tutions that will afford a reasonable degree of security coupled with a reasonable degree of personal liberty. It was done in Philadelphia, and then and there the theory became an established fact.

To be sure, it took many years and a long series of varied tests to establish the durability of the work; but a century and a half later no doubt remains—the thing has stood the test of time and of repeated, terrific assaults. It was sound and strong. It was far better, indeed, than even the cheerful old philosopher who hailed the rising sun could make himself believe.

The optimism of the modern American, a reflection of his self-confidence, tries his friends in Europe sorely, and has gone far to make us a thoroughly disliked people. To the extent that it is based on mere complacency over the American's advantageous position in the twentieth century it is an unattractive trait which no man of sense approves; and it is not to be denied that in a great many instances it is mere complacency.

But it wasn't complacency in Philadelphia in the closing decade of the eighteenth century. A shoestring country on the edge of a continental wilderness, viewed with suspicion by all the ancient monarchies and with open hostility by most of them, had nothing to be complacent about. Nevertheless, those people were optimistic. They believed in the capacity of men to govern themselves better than they could be governed by kings, and they were setting out to prove it. A man who is about to put to the test of experiment an untried theory is optimistic or apprehensive according to the strength of his belief in the theory. Philadelphia believed its theory strongly, not merely the great men who were running the government but the businessmen, the workmen, the women, and the children, as well.

Its optimism, therefore, was not complacency, it was faith. Some people couldn't see it then. Of the fifty-five delegates who wrote the Constitution, sixteen refused to sign the thing, and they undoubtedly regarded the faith of the rest as fatuous. But, with the advantage of hindsight, all the world can see now that it was magnificent, one of the imponderables that, far more than size, or wealth, or material splendor, make a city great.

So it has come about that the little city of less than thirty thousand people, now swallowed up in a vast urban region containing nearly as many people as the whole United States had in 1790, still dominates the imagination of men.

A man's city consists, to begin with, of the place where he lives and the place where he works; after that, but less definitely his own, are the place where he plays and, if he is pious, the place where he prays. But beyond these strictly personal interests, a man's city is not really land and houses nor the great majority of the people in the houses, for to most of them he is completely indifferent. One's city is not anything material but the vast complex of memorable things

HAYM SOLOMON ADVANCING
NEEDED FUNDS TO ROBERT MORRIS
TO FINANCE THE REVOLUTION

~~~~~~

that the city has seen and is seeing; which is to say, it consists for the most part of the deeds of illustrious citizens who have lived or are living in it, and for a lesser part, of the customs, traditions, and manner of living of the anonymous masses who have lived and are living there. Naturally, not all these are of equal importance; the most notable among them will constitute the greater part of the city as it exists, not in a geographical area, but in the minds and hearts of men.

In this sense, the greater Philadelphia is not the industrial and commercial giant that sprawls far beyond the Schuylkill and for many miles up and down the Delaware; not the financial power whose banks, insurance companies, and security dealers handle a tremendous proportion of the money of the nation; not even the four million people who inhabit the city and the urban region immediately adjacent to it.

THE COUNTRY'S FIRST AND GREATEST
PRESIDENT ALSO KNEW HOW TO DINE
IN HIS PHILADELPHIA HOUSE

The greater Philadelphia is the city of Independence Hall and the Liberty Bell, the city where the Declaration of Independence and the Constitution were written, the city where the astonishing Muhlenberg parsons preached for a while and fought for a while, and played politics awhile, where Frederick A. C. Muhlenberg, as first Speaker of the House, started the legislative branch on its long career while Washington was starting the executive branch and John Jay the judiciary.

Philadelphia is Franklin, with his books and his kites and his lightning rods and his jokes in the middle of everything. It is Charles Willson Peale, mingling his stuffed animals with paintings of presidents and gods and goddesses. It is Abigail Adams and Mrs. Oldmixon, and incomparable Dolley (she insisted on that "e") whom "the great little Madison" snatched away from Philadelphia to a dazzling career in Washington. It is the twenty-eight thousand whose names we do not know but whose courage, cheerfulness, and confidence in the future sustained and encouraged the great men. It is the city where faith and works, because they walked hand in hand, each had life and had it more abundantly.

This city overshadows the gigantic port of modern times because all the cargoes in the world do not impress men as much as they are impressed by courage and faith. Especially is it attractive in times as perilous and perplexed as those in which the republic started on its way. When the twentieth century was half gone the United States of America once more found the path ahead dark and beset with difficulties, as difficult and uncertain as it was when the eighteenth century drew to a close. There are enemies abroad, there are faint hearts and faltering hands at home, and the past offers no precedent on which we can rely for guidance.

In these circumstances, who does not look with delight on old Philadelphia? It is one of the finest of our possessions, for it is a reminder that this sort of thing has happened before, yet Americans proved that they were equal to it. For every black care that rides our backs, they had an equivalent, or worse; yet, armed with faith and courage and cheerful hearts, they came through.

While we have that memory in mind, we too are somewhat armed. Knowing the outcome of what those men did, it is possible for a modern American, wandering through Independence Hall, to contemplate the President's chair with the old philosopher's eyes, and see there the symbol of a rising, not a setting sun.